BUNGALOW BASICS
LIVING ROOMS

By Paul Duchscherer
Photography by Douglas Keister

Pomegranate
SAN FRANCISCO

Published by Pomegranate Communications, Inc.
Box 808022, Petaluma, California 94975
800-227-1428; www.pomegranate.com

Pomegranate Europe Ltd.
Unit 1, Heathcote Business Centre, Hurlbutt Road
Warwick, Warwickshire CV34 6TD, U. K.
(44) 01926 430111

Library of Congress Cataloging-in-Publication Data
Duchscherer, Paul.
    Bungalow basics. Living rooms / by Paul Duchscherer ; photography by
Douglas Keister.
        p. cm.
    ISBN 0-7649-2494-X
    1. Bungalows. 2. Living rooms. 3. Arts and crafts movement–United States. I.
Title: Living rooms. II. Keister, Douglas. III. Title.

    NA7571.D823 2003
    728'.373–dc21

                                                                    2003042990

Pomegranate Catalog No. A678

Designed by Patrice Morris

Printed in Korea

12 11 10 09 08 07 06 05 04 03   10 9 8 7 6 5 4 3 2 1

This book is dedicated to the discovery,
appreciation, and preservation of bungalows,
and especially to all those who
love and care for them.

Acknowledgments

Because of space limitations, we regret that it is not possible to acknowledge each of those individuals and organizations who have helped us with this book. Our heartfelt appreciation is extended especially to all the homeowners who, by graciously sharing their homes with us, have made this book a reality. Special thanks are given also to Sandy Schweitzer, John Freed, and Don Merrill for their tireless support, unflagging encouragement, and invaluable assistance. We salute you!

At the end of the book, we have noted a few of the talented artisans, architects, designers, craftspeople, and manufacturers whose work appears here, but space constraints preclude us from crediting each one. We offer them all our deepest gratitude. Alternatively, our readers may wish to consult the extensive credit listings in our earlier book series, published by Penguin Putnam Inc. (comprising *The Bungalow: America's Arts & Crafts Home*, *Inside the Bungalow: America's Arts & Crafts Interior*, and *Outside the Bungalow: America's Arts & Crafts Garden*), which make reference to many of the images that are also included in this book.

BUNGALOW BASICS

Developers and builders of bungalows knew the importance of "curb appeal" and usually did whatever they could to enhance it. They also knew that many prospective home-owners, once they opened the wide front door and stepped inside, would immediately think, "This is it!" Such was the ability of a well-appointed bungalow living room to disarm resistance.

To elicit those decisive first impressions, the living room was likely to have more square footage than any other room. And, since a hall-mark of bungalow planning was the relationship between the living and dining rooms, there were likely to be in view upon entry not just one but two generous rooms, making the whole house feel bigger than it really was (Figures 7, 14). Instead of wasting space on hall-ways, most plans used the living and dining rooms as circulation space, a reaction to the compartmentalized layouts of Victorian-era houses. These simple innovations added to the bungalow's appeal.

In addition to the dining room and front porch—touted by period tastemakers as "the outdoor living room," for it offered spillover space for large gatherings (Figures 3–4)—some bungalows had an extra room adjoining the living room, commonly called a den (Figures 9, 15, 17). This "bonus" space might have been separated by only an open doorway (as with the dining room) or sometimes by a pocket door (Figure 14). Dens served a variety of uses. Built-ins such as bookcases and desks could define a den as a study, a library, or both (Figures 19, 36–37). Most dens could function also as a music room, sewing room, hobby room, children's playroom, or an occasional guestroom.

The primary focal point of a bungalow living room was its fireplace. Usually placed to be visible upon entry (Figures 2, 8), fireplaces varied greatly in finish, materials, and appearance. The Craftsman style, with its emphasis on natural materials, favored wood mantels. Sometimes paneling above the mantel incorporated a mirror and wall sconces (Figure 30). Structural elements were often exposed, perhaps appearing only below the mantel shelf or also as a massive chimney rising to the ceiling (Figures 16, 28, 35).

The most popular materials for Craftsman-style fireplaces were river rock (also called cobble) and roughly textured fieldstone (Figures 2, 29, 33), usually obtained locally. With its many varieties (and typically lower cost), brick was the most widespread fireplace material. Clinker brick, with a craggy texture and deep coloring, was a classic Craftsman material (Figure 12). Plain brick, in muted shades of buff, brown, or red (Figures 26–27, 45), was more common; sometimes, for interest, colors and textures were mixed (Figure 28). Ceramic tile was also used for fireplace surrounds (Figures 8, 11, 20). Tile with an irregular or handcrafted quality was often preferred (Figures 6–7, 23, 34, 47).

Bungalow living rooms were a primary place to find built-in

cabinetry, often centered around the fireplace. A roomwide mantel was a popular solution to the dilemma of what to do with the fireplace wall (Figures 11, 26). This space-efficient arrangement usually included bookcases with glass doors to either side of the fireplace (Figures 6, 34). Some had built-in benches instead of bookcases (Figures 2, 10, 30) or a cabinet on one side and a bench on the other (Figures 7, 27, 47). Drop-front desks were occasionally part of fireplace-wall built-ins (Figure 22). Many bungalow fireplaces had two small windows, sometimes with art-glass panels (Figure 34), to either side of the chimney, above the height of the mantel (Figures 6, 11). Some plans gave fireplaces special prominence by placing them in a recessed alcove, called an inglenook, with built-in seating to either side (Figure 17).

Handcrafted metalwork was a classic Arts and Crafts design medium; some period examples are truly works of art. Living room metalwork usually pertained to the fireplace, most frequently (other than fire tools) as smoke guards or hoods. These ranged in size from tiny to towering and were, in some cases, the most interesting thing about the fireplace (Figures 20–21, 27, 34, 38). Hammered copper was favored in the Craftsman era; iron and steel were also used, sometimes in combination with copper (Figure 10).

Beamed ceilings are closely associated with Craftsman-style interiors, although some living rooms featured a substantial perimeter crown molding rather than beams (Figures 7, 11, 14, 26). Others might not have had any molding at the ceiling but instead molding that linked the tops of the doors and windows (Figure 40). While some ceiling beams really were structural in nature (Figures 1, 28), most exposed beams in bungalow interiors were nonstructural. Some were stylized into flattened, linear design elements (Figures 8, 21, 25). Most common were those called box beams (because they were hollow, like a box); their open tops were placed against the ceiling, leaving the bottom and two sides visible (Figures 2, 16, 20).

Separate from their construction, the most interesting thing about beamed ceilings was their arrangement within a room. They could be used to manipulate a room's proportions (Figure 24). They could help conceal visual flaws (Figure 4), draw attention to a fireplace (Figure 30), or make a connection to an adjoining room. Some beams framed the perimeter of the ceiling (Figures 20, 35) or completely covered it like a grid (Figures 2, 9, 16), while others ran in only one direction (Figures 17, 21, 29–30, 47). Most dramatic were living rooms that used beams in combination with high-peaked ceilings, particularly those finished entirely in wood (Figures 28, 31–34).

Beams were sometimes mounted with lighting fixtures (Figure 25), which might add sparkle from intentionally bare lightbulbs placed at beam intersections (Figure 8) or lanterns hanging from chains (Figures 2, 16, 21). A fairly common lighting choice was a simple, suspended glass bowl (Figure 11). Other fixtures featured small glass-shaded lights or lanterns, suspended from a central point or ceiling-mounted backplate (Figures 19–20, 27–28, 31, 36, 47). For atmospheric lighting, wall sconces were popular (Figures 2, 7, 9, 18, 24–25, 27, 30–33). A more costly (and thus less common) option was to have custom-designed fixtures (Figures 22–23).

Although some bungalow living and dining rooms occupied a single undivided space, they were more commonly separated by a large opening—at least as wide as a double door—preserving maximum sight lines between the rooms (Figures 21, 29). Such openings usually had wood casings around them that matched those elsewhere, but not always (Figure 5). Some openings were almost as wide as the room (Figure 7). Especially typical of Craftsman-era bungalows, sliding pocket doors allowed for more flexible uses of the rooms on either side. Some pocket doors had glass panes (sometimes beveled) like French doors (Figure 11). Later bungalows from the 1920s were more likely to have swinging French doors instead of pocket doors.

Another popular way to divide the living and dining rooms was with a colonnade, a pair of columns supported by low walls set within a wide opening. Colonnades—which, like other built-in features, could be ordered from catalogs (Figure 13)—implied a sense of separation yet maintained openness between the rooms (Figures 15–16). Many of the walls supporting the columns had built-in cabinets (which usually opened toward the living room). The shape and size of the columns varied. Those influenced by the Craftsman style were square, tapered, or trapezoidal (Figure 14), while those displaying a Colonial Revival influence were round and turned, like classical columns (Figure 12).

Portières (door draperies) were very popular in bungalows; traces of their existence can be detected in the doorways of many living and dining rooms (Figure 21). Adding a textile's softness and color to a room (Figure 3), portières also provided privacy, muffled sound, and blocked drafts. Frequently used in combination with wide pocket doors (and sometimes on single doors), they usually appeared only in the "public" rooms.

In most matters of decoration, the living room was given the highest priority and biggest budget of any room in the house. It had to function as the family's main gathering space, as well as a suitable reception and entertainment room for visitors. Design advice was available in abundance from books and popular magazines. For those drawn to the Craftsman style, a magazine called *The Craftsman,* published (from 1901 to 1916) by the famous furniture manufacturer Gustav Stickley, promoted the bungalow as America's most ideal "simple" home. More mainstream magazines, such as *House Beautiful* and *House and Garden,* also instructed bungalow owners in matters of taste and style.

Color schemes for bungalow living rooms during the Craftsman era tended toward warm, earthy colors that complemented the tones of the woodwork (Figures 2–3, 5, 26). Wall colors in general were most likely to be of medium values, with warm neutrals being the most popular and versatile. Sometimes more adventurous schemes appeared that used vivid shades of red, blue, or green (Figures 14, 27, 39). However, the deeper "jewel tones" were typically reserved as accent colors for pillows, draperies, upholstery, and carpets. Oriental-style rugs were popular, but many period illustrations show that simple, solid-color area carpets (most with restrained border designs) were probably almost as prevalent (Figures 1, 3, 5, 17, 38–39). Native American rugs were also considered appropriate to the Craftsman style (Figures 2, 12, 33, 40).

Most bungalows featured a fairly inexpensive wood (like fir), which was usually stained a dark color to even out the irregular figuring of its grain (Figures 14, 16). If the budget permitted, a better-quality wood (such as quartersawn oak or mahogany) might be used (Figures 2, 19–20, 22–23, 34). While natural woodwork was the norm for living and dining rooms, woodwork in the "private" and "utilitarian" areas of the house often was painted a light color like cream or white, thought to be more "hygienic." Some later bungalow interiors from the 1920s—particularly those influenced by the Colonial Revival style—originally had light-painted woodwork throughout. In Craftsman living rooms, walls sometimes were paneled to the ceiling (Figures 18, 21, 30–31). Wainscoting—partial-height paneling, usually capped by a plate rail—was less typical of living rooms than dining rooms, but occasionally it was used in both (Figures 14, 29, 35).

With regard to living room furnishings, most people had a mix of styles (usually by default) rather than a roomful of Craftsman-style pieces. Often a suite of overstuffed furniture provided primary seating, accompanied by various occasional tables, lighter-weight chairs, and footstools. The built-in window seats or fireside benches in many bungalows reduced the need for much extra seating and also offered handy storage inside. Considerable space could be taken up by the various ways that music was brought into the middle-class home. Pianos were usually the upright variety; some households had automated player pianos. Record players (such as the Victrola) were convenient for enjoying recorded music at home; by the 1920s, radios, often housed in large cabinets, were quickly becoming a standard presence in most American living rooms.

Wallpaper competed with paint and special hand-painted finishes such as stenciling, sponging, and glazing (Figures 5, 14, 22–23, 41) as the preferred choice for overall wall treatments of bungalow living rooms. Some wallpapers imitated hand-painted effects or other materials (Figures 17, 19). Simple textiles such as linen or burlap were occasionally used as wall coverings (Figure 40), most likely set into panels for easier installation. However, a living room's most important decorative feature was often a frieze around the top of the room. The Arts and Crafts ideal of bringing elements of nature indoors was reflected in the use of landscape friezes (Figures 38, 42). More geometric designs, such as so-called pendant friezes, were also allied with the Craftsman aesthetic (Figures 17, 45, 47).

The lion's share of the bungalow's best qualities and features could be found in its living room: a flickering fire, an absence of clutter because of built-in furnishings, daylight streaming through the mellowing filter of art glass, fresh air circulating through open windows, and nature close at hand by way of doors leading to the front porch, terrace, or garden. The collective attributes of the bungalow made it a wonder for its time. That its early-twentieth-century innovations still afford such comfortable conditions for today's bungalow dwellers attests to the enduring values of hearth and home. These values, and the continuing appeal of the Craftsman lifestyle, are reflected in the following photographs, from then and now.

❧ 1. This living room was featured in a 1921 plan book called *Building with Assurance,* published by the Morgan Woodwork Company. Rather than the more common box beams, these beams appear to be true structural elements of solid wood. The composition of this view closely resembles that of Figure 3, although here a fireplace abuts the built-in bench, creating a partial inglenook effect.

❦ 2. The living room of the 1909
Keyes bungalow in Altadena, California–
listed on the National Register of Historic
Places–is entered from the front porch
through a wide, beveled glass door.
Built-in benches flank the stone-faced
fireplace. The quartersawn oak woodwork used throughout the room inspired
the muted palette of earthy paint colors,
creating a subtle harmony between the
architecture and collection of fine period
furnishings and Native American textiles.

🐝 3. In this illustration from a 1920s catalog of the Olson Rug Company, an easy flow between indoors and outdoors is suggested by the French doors leading to a covered porch. The warm wall color and use of various textiles (pillows, table runner, patterned curtains and matching portières) soften the room. Exuding simplicity, an unpatterned, nubby-textured carpet, in a warm neutral color, provides softness underfoot.

🐝 4. A well-furnished front porch expands this living room's feeling of spaciousness. Through French doors at left, a glass-enclosed side porch can be opened to living room activities or closed off for separate uses. Behind a Gustav Stickley settle in the corner alcove, the large window's transom can be opened for added ventilation. Strategically placed box beams emphasize the room's width and help offset its slightly irregular shape.

✾ 5. This atmospheric rendering from an early-twentieth-century paint manufacturer's catalog demonstrates how color schemes between adjoining rooms can vary significantly yet still work in harmony. Also promoted is stenciled decoration, used here to accent an uncased arched opening and various other architectural elements. Created by sponging or ragging techniques (which sometimes blend colors), textured paint finishes are another idea recommended here.

🐝 **6.** Between a pair of built-in bookcases with leaded glass doors, the fireplace has a surround of Batchelder tiles with a matte-glazed, leathery finish. The two small windows above are a typical bungalow feature. The configuration of the "Chicago window" at right, so called because of its prevalent use in many of that city's early skyscrapers, has a larger, fixed central panel, flanked by two smaller, openable windows, which provide flexible control of air circulation.

7. Seen from the front door, this long view of adjoining living and dining rooms maximizes the feeling of spaciousness for a small house. A pair of low walls (whose ends resemble square pedestals) are set within the nearly roomwide opening. An asymmetrical arrangement of built-ins around the fireplace includes the bench at right and a lit display cabinet with leaded glass doors. With their handmade look, the mottled blue-green fireplace tiles complement the room's period furnishings and Native American textiles.

🐝 8. The style of this home is Craftsman, but the sleek lines of its living room suggest some of the crisp spareness and overt horizontality of the Prairie style. The effect is enhanced by flattened ceiling beams accented by bare lightbulbs at their intersections. Inset with art-glass panels, a wide front door and side-lights are recent replacements that look quite at home: the door's trio of small openings above a tall vertical one makes a well-proportioned composition.

9. With the living room at its heart, this home's plan has an appealing sequence of flowing spaces. A small den/library (through a wide doorway in the far corner) encloses one end of the front porch. Grouped together as one unit (and parallel to the porch) are four casement windows fitted with Roman shades. Less typical of bungalow floor plans, a separate entry hall opens to this room through another wide doorway (flanked by wall sconces) at far right.

🐨 10. This living room in a 1911 Los Angeles bungalow enjoys light from three sides. Designed by Vawter and Walker, its thoughtful planning and red-wood detailing remain remarkably fresh. An original feature above the fireplace is a whimsical low-relief scene of a pipe-playing figure under trees. Carved into the brick by sculptor John Stanbough Souther, the panel unites art and architecture. Seat cushions rest atop the brick extensions on either side.

🐝 11. Providing access from either the dining room (in the foreground) or the entry hall (at left), wide doorways fitted with beveled glass-paned pocket doors add flexibility to this light-filled living room. Under boldly scaled crown moldings, the roomwide fireplace mantel incorporates double sets of built-in bookcases, now used to display art pottery. Derived from the matte-glazed fireplace tiles, the warm color of the walls was given extra depth and texture by a rag-painting technique.

❧ 12. *(left)* Through an open doorway with a colonnade (whose round, turned columns suggest a Colonial Revival influence), the cozy clinker brick fireplace and built-in seating at right create an inviting retreat. Dens offer many potential uses: as an expansion space for living room activities or as a library, a music room, or possibly a guestroom (although dens with closeable doors are more likely to be appropriated for extra sleeping space).

❧ 13. *(above)* In this 1921 catalog illustration from the Morgan Company, a colonnade separates a living room and dining room. Craftsman-style columns are usually square and tapered, but they vary widely in height and proportion. The Morgan Company supplied doors, moldings, and other prefabricated built-ins (like colonnades) that reduced on-site construction costs.

🐝 14. A colonnade with built-in cabinets allows openness between this living room and the dining room beyond, yet each area maintains its individual identity. Copied from surviving fragments, the wall's mottled finish re-creates the original paint scheme. A den is located behind the wide pocket door at right. When closed off, it can become a private guestroom or study; when open, it expands the living room space and overlooks a fireplace on the opposite wall (out of view, far left).

🐾 15. Although still visually a part of the living room, this den/library alcove feels separate, thanks to the colonnade set into its broad opening. The alcove has tall built-in bookcases to either side of the windows. Under them is a built-in window seat that invites browsing or reading. Above the bookcases and windows, a striking wallpaper frieze reproduces a work by famous British designer-illustrator Walter Crane that was first shown at the 1900 Paris Exhibition.

🦌 **16.** Seen through a colonnade from the dining room, this perspective of a 1907 living room includes the den/library alcove (at far left) shown in Figure 15. In an unusual planning twist, the front door opens into a narrow entry hall (lined with a window seat) that runs behind the step-sided clinker brick fireplace. To the left of the fireplace, the dark outline of the front door can be seen through the open slats of a built-in screen.

🐝 17. From the 1916–1917 catalog of James Davis Artistic Paperhangings, this illustration shows wallpapers that replicate the effects of hand-painted finishes and stenciling. Between the living room and the den (at right) is a wide opening fitted with pocket doors. An inglenook (at left) further expands the feeling of spaciousness. Both a Craftsman influence (in the beamed ceiling, built-ins, and earthy color palette) and a Colonial Revival influence (in the furniture forms and some of the woodwork detailing) are apparent.

🐝 18. Damage to this part of the Cohen-Bray House in Oakland, California, caused by the 1906 San Francisco earthquake provided the opportunity to create this classic Craftsman-style interior. In contrast, the other primary rooms of the 1884 Stick/Eastlake-style house retain most of their original decorative schemes. Although descendants of the original owners still occupy this important house, it is now also the headquarters of the Victorian Preservation Center of Oakland and is open to the public.

❧ 19. In addition to its original embossed wallpaper frieze, this den/library retains its original built-ins, quartersawn oak-paneled walls, and stepped corbels pegged with ebony accents. Derived from Chinese furniture forms, the "cloud lift" motif appears in variations on the drop-front desk and in the bookcase doors. These details suggest that the architects and builders of this 1911 Los Angeles house, John and Daniel Althouse, were likely inspired by the work of Greene and Greene.

20. Adjoining the den/library in Figure 19 (seen through the doorway at left), the living room also shows the Greenes' influence, in its elegant Honduran mahogany woodwork and ebony-pegged detailing. Typical bungalow features like the wainscot paneling, fireplace, and box-beamed ceiling are elevated here to the quality of fine furniture. An original hand-hammered copper hood blends well with the matte-glazed, leatherlike finish of the fireplace's Grueby tile.

❦ 21. Entirely paneled in redwood, this living room exudes a warmth that only natural wood can provide. Designed by noted San Francisco Bay Area architect Louis Christian Mullgardt, the 1907 Evans House in Marin County, California, retains most of its original interior finishes, including an embossed burlap-textured wallpaper with a metallic gold finish (intended to reflect light, but now age-darkened) between the ceiling beams. Old brass hardware awaits replacement of the original draperies and portières. Opposite the large copper-hooded fireplace, French doors open to a deck that is also accessible from the dining room beyond.

❧ 22 & 23. The living room of the Thorsen House in Berkeley, California (1908–1910) is a masterwork by celebrated architects (and brothers) Charles and Henry Greene. Handcrafted entirely of Honduran mahogany, the room's woodwork displays variations of the architects' favored "cloud lift" motif. Instead of the more typical hanging lanterns, the Greenes designed unusual recessed art-glass ceiling fixtures for this room. Hand-painted flowering branches, attributed to Charles Greene, accent the wooden forms dividing the frieze. Other signature details include the bold steel elements framing the fireplace opening and the tiny mosaic accents in the Grueby tile surround. The room appears here as staged for a 1996 benefit exhibition for ongoing restoration of the Thorsen House, which, since 1943, has been home to the Sigma Phi Society (a college fraternity). Many of the home's original carpets, artworks, and architect-designed furnishings (including the fireside bench and oval library table) were returned for display in the exhibition.

🐝 24. The 1909 Randell House in Berkeley, California, has a living room ceiling that uses differently sized beams to suggest separate areas within the overall space. A pair of deeper beams span the width of the room, emphasizing its central portion; they also reinforce a cross-axial relationship between the large recessed fireplace and an angled bay window alcove on the opposite wall. Smaller sitting areas at either end of the room are also defined by the crossbeams.

🐾 25. This bright and spacious living room enjoys direct access to the garden through a pair of French doors. Designed by Pasadena architect Alfred Heineman (and constructed in partnership with his brother Arthur), the 1909 Los Angeles house has handsome original woodwork of Port Orford cedar, noted for its exceptional durability and pest resistance. Beneath wide and shallow box beams, wide planks of the beautiful wood are used to create the frieze.

🐝 26. Brightly lit from three sides because of the house's U-shaped floor plan, this 1911 living room faces a small courtyard at right. In a variation of the so-called Chicago window (see Figure 6), the arrangement at right incorporates three small transoms across its top. Along with the reproductions of Stickley furniture, the simple linear motifs in the fireplace brickwork and in the glass doors of the bookcases still appear surprisingly modern today.

🐛 27. Found under old wallpaper, a deep terra-cotta color has returned to the walls of this 1906 living room, with all its original built-ins and lighting fixtures. On the fireplace, stepped brick corbels support the thick mantel shelf and add depth to the otherwise plain brickwork. Another original feature is the hand-made copper fireplace hood, made more unusual by a curious pair of cast metal designs resembling winged mythological beasts.

🐾 **28.** Although its floor plan also includes a more traditional living room, a 1920s bungalow enjoys the added bonus of this rather informal living area at its heart. Seen here from the entry hall, it also functions as circulation space between other first-floor areas: the kitchen is to the left; two bedrooms and a bathroom are through the far corner door. Reached by a dramatic open stairway, a finished attic level with two more bedrooms and a second bathroom makes this house larger than it appears. Positioned between pairs of French doors to a patio and garden, a massive brick fireplace with a hoodlike chimney rises to a peaked wooden ceiling with exposed structural beams.

🐌 29. The beauty of this room was once nearly obliterated by years of abuse and neglect. Previously stuccoed over, the gracefully arched stone fireplace has been restored, with a new keystone inscribed with "1909" (the home's construction date) placed at its center. The geometric leaded glass window detailing, board-and-batten wainscoting, and shallow box beams all had to be re-created.

🐚 30. The pair of recessed windows to either side of this living room's fireplace are fitted with useful built-in bookcases and window seats. Another original feature that dates to 1905 is the fireplace surround and hearth, which are faced with thick, matte-glazed terra-cotta tiles with a mottled finish. Helping expand the room's width and offset its length, two box beams aligned with the fireplace divide the ceiling into three parts.

❦ 31. Redwood is the finish material for all the wall and ceiling surfaces of the living and dining rooms in the Kenfield House, a Berkeley, California, bungalow built about 1905. With its French doors folded back, the wide opening at left creates a more flowing sense of space. Although the sloping ceilings mirror the actual angle of the roof, less refined structural elements are concealed within the box beams.

🐚 32. The living room of San Diego's 1933 Roper House, designed by noted architect Cliff May, includes many rustic effects typical of the Spanish Colonial Revival style: distressed, exposed dark timber framing, thick adobe-like walls, a corner "beehive" fireplace, and use of wrought iron. Cliff May is better known for his part in the development of the California Ranch House style, a major influence on post-World War II tract housing across the country.

🦋 **33**. A recent remodel has given a greater feeling of spaciousness and light to this Pasadena bungalow's living room, which now has a beamed, peaked wooden ceiling. Once the former flat ceiling was removed, a pair of windows, detailed to match adjacent originals, were inserted above the fireplace. Because the roof's structural elements were never intended to be seen, they required a cladding in new finish-grade wood. In a careful reconstruction, the old river rock fireplace was enlarged to better fit the room's new proportions.

🐝 34. Seen from the vantage of pocket doors that connect it to a larger living room, this room is actually a den/library in a large 1912 Craftsman-style home in Los Angeles. Luminous "feather-grain" mahogany woodwork is especially show-cased in the peaked ceiling's box beams. In color harmony with the wood and muted fireplace tile surround are the finely crafted art glass of the landscape-scene windows, the more geometric bookcase doors, and the subtle burlap wall covering.

🐝 35. This room's mix of stylistic sensibilities probably reflects the personal tastes of the original owners who built the bungalow in 1915. Its woodwork detailing and all-wood box-beamed ceiling are almost aggressively Craftsman; the oversized fireplace ensemble suggests a Spanish influence; and the ornate ceiling fixture and matching sconces have an oddly baroque character. Despite this unlikely mix, the carpet and wallpaper inject some unifying color. Art-glass pocket doors open to the dining room at right.

🐝 36. Open to the living room in Figure 35, this den is fitted with a built-in corner bench, glass-fronted bookcase, and drop-front desk, all of which create a compact study/library. Like the rest of this house's built-ins, fittings, and fixtures (and even its plans), the art glass was probably ordered from a catalog. Its stylized landscape scenes recall illustrations in children's books from the same period.

❧ 37. A drop-front desk unit and coordinating pair of bookcases numbered among the Morgan Company's many offerings of prefabricated built-in cabinetry, as shown in this illustration from their 1921 catalog, *Building With Assurance*. Upgraded with leaded glass doors, these components could either outfit a bungalow's living room or make a small den into more of a study or library. The window seat at right allows for books to be stowed along its length.

❧ 38. From Henry Collins Brown's 1912 book, *Home Building and Decoration*, this room embodies an Arts and Crafts ideal of bringing elements of nature indoors. The landscape frieze makes a literal reference, while the area rug's border uses more abstracted motifs from nature. The reddish colors of the copper fireplace hood, curtains, and walls complement the cool blue-gray of the fireplace tile and the various green shades of the frieze, carpet border, upholstery, and library tabletop. Binding everything together are the deep tones of the woodwork and furniture.

🐝 39. From a promotional postcard distributed in the 1910s by the Macey Furniture Company, this image is more interesting for its color scheme than for its furniture (although the modular, stacking bookcases show an enduringly practical concept). Rich shades of red on the walls, carpet field, and curtains are offset by more subdued greens and blues in the fireplace tile, chimney, and carpet border (where they are mixed with gold). The lighting, beams, curving bracket, and wainscot are Craftsman in style; the diamond-paned windows and form of the chimney suggest English inspiration.

🐾 40. In a renovation of "Mariposa" (formerly the Frost-Tufts House), this former bedroom was converted to a den/library. Although natural woodwork survives elsewhere in the 1911 Hollywood house, it was painted here to avoid any contrasts with the new built-in bookcases and cabinetry. In the frieze area, the original wall treatment of natural burlap has been re-created and used to conceal stereo speakers. Period furnishings and scattered Navajo rugs lend the room warmth.

🐝 41. Although the house itself was built around 1912, this den/library was added in 1921 as part of a renovation by noted Berkeley, California, architect John Hudson Thomas. French doors opening to a shallow balcony admit light and air. Parts of the lower wall areas still have their original painted finish, a mottled texture blending a dull blue with a yellow-ochre color that harmonizes with the wood.

🐝 42. This cheerful Craftsman-style living room adjoins an open dining area, both the result of a recent remodel that combined smaller spaces. Like the period designs that inspired it, a new hand-painted landscape frieze takes motifs from nature–here, birch trees and rolling hills–to evoke a sense of the outdoors. To minimize the impact of the beam in the foreground (a vestige of the remodel and a structural necessity), the frieze design continues onto both of its sides.

🐝 43. In a tradition of the English Arts and Crafts movement, the art-glass panels in this den/study incorporate a quotation from Chaucer's *Legend of Good Women* on a banner, unfurling between stylized grapevine motifs. Below, related designs on the stenciled curtains and an embroidered pillow echo those motifs. Other references to England include the William Morris wallpaper and the border with Tudor roses.

🐝 44 & 45. Before and after views of this living room show how the thoughtful addition of period-appropriate patterns and colors can add architectural interest and improve proportions. The goal was to transform the white-walled room into a more sympathetic background for a fine collection of Arts and Crafts-era furnishings. Because the owners preferred to keep the color palette light, a small-scale leafy pattern, in pale shades of yellow and green, has been used on the primary wall areas. In the absence of picture molding, a narrow paper border divides the lower walls from the frieze area above them; similar borders panelize the upper face and sides of the fireplace to the ceiling. Reproduced from a 1910s design (the house dates to 1913), the "pendant" frieze lends scale and rhythm to the room.

🐝 46 & 47. Before and after views of this living room illustrate why the common choice of white walls is not necessarily effective with dark-stained woodwork. The owners wanted to integrate the room's Craftsman architectural features into a warmer and more appropriate design scheme. The solution was to use period-style wallpapers in a deeper color palette—mostly a shade of green popular in the Craftsman era, with rich accents of gold and purple. A printed "burlap" pattern in a light-reflective metallic-gold finish covers the panels between the ceiling beams, with a narrow border framing each panel. The same borders frame a "pendant" frieze. To create a simpler background for artwork and furnishings, the lower walls are papered in an overall pattern of small leaves. Now, the fireplace has a newfound prominence, the old built-ins blend in seamlessly, new curtains brighten the windows, and all the period furnishings look completely at home.

BUNGALOW BACKGROUND

America's most popular house of the early twentieth century, the bungalow, is making a big comeback as our newest "historic" house. Surviving bungalows are now considered treasures by historic preservationists, while homeowners rediscover the bungalow's appeal as a modest, practical home with a convenient floor plan. This book highlights an important aspect of bungalow interiors.

Webster's New Collegiate Dictionary describes a bungalow as "a dwelling of a type first developed in India, usually one story, with low sweeping lines and a wide verandah." The word *bungalow* derives from the Hindi *bangala,* both an old Hindu kingdom in the Bengal region of India and a rural Bengali hut with a high thatched-roof overhang creating a covered porch (or verandah) around the perimeter to provide shade from the scorching sun. The height and steep pitch of the roof encouraged the hottest air to rise and escape, while cooler air flowed in at ground level (especially after sundown). The British colonists adapted the design in their own dwellings, and their success spread the concept from India to elsewhere in the British Empire, especially Southeast Asia, Africa, New Zealand, and Australia. By the late eighteenth century, the name *bangala* had been anglicized to *bungalow.*

This name first appeared in print in the United States in 1880.

Used in an architectural journal, it described a single-story, shingled Cape Cod summerhouse ringed by covered porches. By the 1900s, *bungalow* had become part of our popular vocabulary, at first associated with vacation homes, both seaside and mountain. The bungalow's informality, a refreshing contrast to stuffy Victorian houses, helped fuel its popularity as a year-round home. It had its greatest fame as a modest middle-class house from 1900 to 1930.

Widely promoted, the bungalow was touted for its modernity, practicality, affordability, convenience, and often-artistic design. Expanding industry and a favorable economy across the country created an urgent need for new, affordable, middle-class housing, which the bungalow was just in time to meet.

In America, a bungalow implied a basic plan, rather than a specific style, of modest house. Typically, it consisted of 1,200 to 1,500 square feet, with living room, dining room, kitchen, two bedrooms, and bathroom all on one level. Some bungalows had roomy attic quarters, but most attics were bare or intended to be developed as the family's needs grew. A bungalow set in a garden fulfilled many Americans' dream of a home of their own.

Widely publicized California bungalows in the early 1900s spawned frenzied construction in booming urban areas across the country. In design, most bungalows built prior to World War I adopted the so-called Craftsman style, sometimes combined with influences from the Orient, the Swiss chalet, or the Prairie style. After the war, public taste shifted toward historic housing styles, and bungalows adapted Colonial Revival, English cottage, Tudor, Mission, and Spanish Colonial Revival features.

Today Craftsman is the style most associated with bungalows. Characterized inside and out by use of simple horizontal lines, Craftsman style relies on the artistry of exposed wood joinery (often visible on front porch detailing). Natural or rustic materials (wood siding, shingles, stone, and clinker brick) are favored. Interiors may be enriched with beamed ceilings, high wainscot paneling, art glass, and hammered copper or metalwork lighting accents.

The word *Craftsman* was coined by prominent furniture manufacturer and tastemaker Gustav Stickley, who used it to label his line of sturdy, slat-backed furniture (also widely known as Mission style), which was influenced by the English Arts and Crafts movement. That movement developed in the mid-nineteenth century as a reaction against the Industrial Revolution. Early leaders such as John Ruskin and William Morris turned to the medieval past for inspiration as they sought to preserve craft skills disappearing in the wake of factory mechanization.

In both the decorative arts (furniture, wallpaper, textiles, glass, metalwork, and ceramics) and architecture, the Arts and Crafts movement advocated use of the finest natural materials to make practical and beautiful designs, executed with skillful handcraftsmanship. One goal was to improve the poor-quality, mass-produced home furnishings available to the rising middle class. Morris and a group of like-minded friends founded a business to produce well-designed, handcrafted goods for domestic interiors. Although the company aspired to make its goods affordable to all, it faced the inevitable conflict between quality and cost. However, its Arts and Crafts example inspired many others in England (and eventually in America) to relearn treasured old craft traditions and continue them for posterity.

As it grew, the movement also became involved in politics, pressing for social reforms. Factory workers trapped in dull, repetitive jobs (with little hope for anything better) were among their chief concerns; they saw the workers' fate as a waste of human potential and talent.

The idealistic and visionary English movement's artistic goals of design reform were more successful than its forays into social reform. Perhaps its greatest success, in both England and the United States, was in giving the public a renewed sense of the value of quality materials, fine craftsmanship, and good design in times of rapid world change.

The Arts and Crafts movement had multiple influences on the American bungalow. The movement arrived here from England in the early 1900s, just as the bungalow was becoming popular. Among its most successful promoters was Elbert Hubbard, founder of the Roycroft Community, a group of artisans producing handmade books and decorative arts inspired by Morris. Hubbard also published two periodicals and sold goods by mail order.

Gustav Stickley was another American inspired by England's important reform movement and soon was expressing this inspiration in the sometimes austere but well-made designs of his Craftsman style. Becoming an influential promoter of the bungalow as an ideal "Craftsman home," he marketed furniture, lighting, metalwork, and textiles styled appropriately for it. His magazine, *The Craftsman,* was a popular vehicle for his ideas and products, and he sold plans for the Craftsman houses he published in his magazine. The wide popularity of his Craftsman style spread the aesthetic sensibilities of the Arts and Crafts movement into countless American middle-class households, making it a growing influence on architecture and decorative arts here. (England in the early twentieth century remarkably had no middle-class housing form comparable to the American bungalow, but Australia has bungalows of that period, inspired by ours, rather than any from Britain.)

Other manufacturers eventually contributed to Stickley's downfall by blatantly copying his ideas and products and eroding his market share. Once Stickley's exclusive brand name, the word *Craftsman* was assimilated into general use and became public property after his bankruptcy in 1916.

Americans choosing the Craftsman style for their homes, interiors, and furnishings rarely were committed to the artistic and philosophical reforms of the Arts and Crafts movement; most were simply following a vogue. Prospective homeowners (and real estate developers) usually selected their bungalow designs from inexpensive sets of plans marketed in catalogs called plan books; few used an architect's services. Some people even bought prefabricated "ready-cut" or "kit" houses. First sold in 1909 by Sears, Roebuck and Company, prefabricated houses soon were widely copied. In the heat of bungalow mania, Sears and others offered tempting incentives to prospective bungalow buyers, such as bonus financing for their lots. For a time, it was said that if you had a job, you could afford a bungalow. But when jobs were in short supply as the Great Depression hit, many defaulted on their little dream homes, leaving their creditors stung.

The depression ended the heyday of the bungalow, but its practical innovations reappeared in later houses, then more likely to be called cottages. The post-World War II ranch house could be considered the legacy of the bungalow. Only recently has a rising demand for lower-cost houses triggered a reevaluation of vintage bungalow stock as viable housing. In response to public demand, the home planning and construction industries have reprised some of the obvious charms of the bungalow in new homes. A real boon for homeowners seeking to restore or renovate a vintage bungalow (or perhaps build a new one) is today's flourishing Arts and Crafts revival, fueled by the demand for a wide array of newly crafted home furnishings that reflect the traditions and spirit of the Arts and Crafts movement. 🦌

CREDITS

Figure 8: Front door designed by Michael Wheelden and made by Larry Word. **Figure 14:** Reproduction of drop-front desk (below picture of water lilies) by Brian Scot Krueger. **Figure 15:** Wallpaper by Bradbury & Bradbury; installed by Peter Bridgman. **Figure 20:** Two landscape paintings (at left) by Chuck Roché. **Figures 22–23:** Exhibition designer: James M. Marrin. **Figure 24:** Pillows by Dianne Ayres, Arts & Crafts Period Textiles. **Figure 26:** Restoration contractor: Elder Vides. **Figure 29:** Renovation architects: The Johnson Partnership, Seattle, Washington. **Figure 30:** Pillows by Dianne Ayres, Arts & Crafts Period Textiles; floor lamp by Sue Johnson. **Figure 33:** Renovation architect: Timothy Anderson, Seattle, Washington. **Figure 35:** Chair with stool by Debey Zito Fine Furniture; wallpaper by Bradbury & Bradbury; installed by Peter Bridgman. **Figure 36:** Chair and table by Debey Zito Fine Furniture; wallpaper by Bradbury & Bradbury; installed by Peter Bridgman. **Figure 40:** Restoration architect: Martin Eli Weill; designer/collection curator: Roger L. Conant. **Figure 42:** Decorative painting by George Zaffle. **Figure 43:** Art glass by Bruce St. John Maher; curtains and pillow by Dianne Ayres, Arts & Crafts Period Textiles; wallpaper and border by Bradbury & Bradbury. **Figure 45:** Wallpaper by Bradbury & Bradbury; installed by Helen Boutell; curtains and pillows by Dianne Ayres, Arts & Crafts Period Textiles. **Figure 47:** Wallpaper by Bradbury & Bradbury installed by Peter Bridgman; curtains and pillows by Dianne Ayres, Arts & Crafts Period Textiles.

ARCHIVAL IMAGES

Figures 1, 5, 13, 37–38: Courtesy the collection of Dianne Ayres and Timothy Hansen, Arts & Crafts Period Textiles. **Figure 39:** Courtesy the collection of Ed Herny. **Figures 3, 17:** From the collection of Paul Duchscherer.